Metamodern Morning Angst and Other Horrors

Selected Poems 2020–2023

by TS S. Fulk

November 11, 2024

ISLAND OF WAK-WAK

Island of Wak-Wak
Örebro, Sweden
www.islandofwakwak.com

Cover Art: *Pyramide de crânes*
by Paul Cézanne, 1901

Typeset using KOMA-Script & $\LaTeX\,2_\varepsilon$.
Printed via IngramSpark.
www.ingramspark.com

ISBN: 978-91-989598-0-2

Contents

Change and Metamorphosis 33

The Horrors of the Cosmos 47

Preface

Not counting my juvenilia in high school, I began writing poetry at university. However, once the grind of work life took over, poems were few and far between. I still wrote fiction and non-fiction, but mostly textbooks. Then right before all the COVID restrictions created a seller's market, I purchased a summer cabin in the North Woods outside of Örebro, Sweden in 2020. The placid sereneness of being surrounded by majestic pines and choruses of birdsong reignited my poetic forge.

The first few poems came slowly, almost painfully, but they came. The birth of online submissions and tracking made finding and submitting to journals a delight. Soon the rejection messages started flooding my inbox. Eventually, as my writing improved and when I started crafting poems for specific journals and theme submissions, the acceptances trickled in.

Since much of my work was specifically tailored for a market, the poetry in this collection is quite varied. However, there are still some overarching categories of poems. This book combines speculative with general poetry starting with ghosts and hauntings; moving to loss, grief, sorrow and healing; morphing into metamorphosis and change; playing with Lovecraftian cosmic horror; and landing with a mix of eclectic speculative poems and musings.

Publishing a collection of poetry is like baring one's soul for the world to judge. I hope you judge it kindly and that the fruit of my summer cabin gives you pleasure, comfort, and solace, despite the horrors herein.

Acknowledgments

"After the Fall" was first published in *Lovecraftiana* Vol. 9, No. 1.

"At a Cabin in the Woods" was first published in 2021 by Wingless Dreamer in *Dreamstones of Summer.*

"Awaiting Persephone" was first published 2023 by Wingless Dreamer in *The Petal Pages.*

"Awstruck" was first published 2022 by MockingOwl Roost in *Special Poetry Issue 2023.*

"By Candlelight" was first published in 2022 by Wingless Dreamer in *Erotica of Eternity.*

"Caged" was first published in *Star*line* Vol. 46, No. 3.

"The Chosen One" was first published in 2021 by Wingless Dreamer in *It's Twelve O'clock.*

"Climate Change" was first published in *Enchanted Conversation: A Fairy Tale Magazine Whispers of Wind* June 2022 Issue.

"A Curse Upon the Land" was first published in 2022 by Rogue Planet Press in *Lovecraftiana* Vol. 7, No. 3.

"Cow Tippin'" was first published in *COW Pure Slush* Vol. 23. June 27, 2022.

"Dream Ghost" was first published in October 2023 in *Cream Scene Magazine.*

"An Elm in Spring" was first published in June 2022 by *The Light Ekphrastic.*

"The Escape" was first published in by *Moss Puppy, Issue 5: Whimsical Woodland.*

"Eternity" was first published in *JOURN-E: The Journal of Imaginative Literature.* Vol. 1, No. 2. Autumnal Equinox (September 2022).

"A False Fresh Start" was first published in *Lothlorien Poetry Journal* October 2022.

"A Fateful Midsummer" was first published in *Siren's Call* Issue 58 Summer 2022.

"A Father's Song" was first published in *Lovecraftiana* Vol. 9, No. 1.

"Five Haiku Written in the Forest" was first published in by *Moss Puppy, Issue 5: Whimsical Woodland.*

"The Forest Wife" was first published in *Lothlorien Poetry Journal* October 2022.

Contents

"Playing Shostakovich's Fifth Symphony, a Bass Trombonist's Perspective" was first published in *Harpy Hybrid Review* Issue 8 "War."

"The Prisoner" was first published in 2022 *Lothlorien Poetry Journal.*

"Recollections of a Wasp" was first published in 2024 by Perennial Press in *Arthropods.*

"The Rise" was first published in 2021 by Wingless Dreamer in *Dawn of the Day.*

"Saintly Motion" was first published in 2021 by Wingless Dreamer in *Snowdrops.*

"Salvage" was first published in *Lothlorien Poetry Journal* October 2022.

"Seeds from Space" was first published in *Star*line* Vol. 44, No. 4.

"The Sinner's Prayer" was first published in 2022 by by Rogue Planet Press in *Lovecraftiana* Vol. 7, No. 3.

"So I'm a Gorgon, and That's Okay" was first published May 2022 in *Primeval Monster.*

"Solving the P'naptuk Paradox" was first published in 2023 by by Rogue Planet Press in *Lovecraftiana* Vol. 8, No. 1.

"Some Philosophical Pondering Over the Nature of Fate" was first published in 2022 in *The Stripes Magazine* Vol. 2, Issue 2.

"Song of the Hunt" was first published in *Lovecraftiana* Vol. 9, No. 1.

"A Sonnet of Healing" was first published in 2023 by Wingless Dreamer in *The Power of Hope.*

"A Sonnet of Questions" was first published in 2022 by Wingless Dreamer in *Field of Black Roses.*

"Starry Night" was first published in 2022 in *The Starry, Starry Night Anthology* by The Ekphrastic Review.

"The Subliminal Lurker" was first published in 2021 by Wingless Dreamer in *Whispers of Pumpkin.*

"Symphony in Yellow" was first published in 2022 by by Rogue Planet Press in *Lovecraftiana* Vol. 7, No. 3.

"The Symphony of Spring" was first published in 2021 by Wingless Dreamer in *Flee to Spring.*

"A Time of Change" was first published in 2023 by Wingless Dreamer in *Wild Heart.*

Contents

"To Cherish and to Hold" was first published in October 2023 in *Cream Scene Magazine*.

"Two Sonnets Smothered in Marmalade" was first published in *Harpy Hybrid Review* Issue 8 "War."

"We Ghouls" was first published in 2022 by by Rogue Planet Press in *Lovecraftiana* Vol. 7, No. 3.

"When I Joined the Living Dead" was first published in 2022 by Wingless Dreamer in *Oxymorons and Poets*.

"Wild Spirits" was first published in 2023 by by Rogue Planet Press in *Lovecraftiana* Vol. 8, No. 1.

Ghostly Hauntings

The Haunting

As always I'm drawn to this spot
where flowers and candles mingle
like teenagers at a disco
just past a tight bend in the path
here in my vivacious forest.
Joggers in their skintight clothing
rush around like commuting cars
unaware of the scenery.

Unaware of the past,
that the candles melt for.
Unaware of the risk
implied in each wilted
bouquet and salt-filled tear
that the stalker has caused.

My spirit flits from tree to tree
waiting for his return.

A Ghost's Sonnet

You haunt me while I rest
in the walls revenant
in the cracks of shadows
from a decaying star
in mist-submerged daydreams
blurred memories of what was

You haunt me while I meander
wandering with a dark purpose
that I'd forgotten long ago
when you burned brightly in my mind
wondering what has inspired you
to appear at that hour of night
a pained bladder or midnight snack
thus we meet when the stars align

You haunt me while I rest
in peace comforted by your warmth

No Closure

I can sense no pattern
in your sporadic haunts
which doesn't surprise me
since you were never one
for regularity
shambles in life and death

Like a wild iris growing
in an immaculate garden
discordant but not unseemly
you were a dissonant contrast
I wish I could have helped you more
but I refused the omen's truth
failing you when you needed me
ignoring your atonal plea

I pray you'll haunt again
so that our souls can rest in peace

After the Crash

I'm just as startled as you are
to see me floating above you
my body is a mangled mess
of broken glass, flesh and metal
the jaws of life cannot help me
because I'm no longer in need
so stop your cursing and swearing
my patience is now eternal

A reflexive shiver
runs brilliant like the sun
through your body and mind
when you see my cleft soul
you look away from me
and focus on the corpse

The ephemeral reflection
in your eye haunts me still

To Cherish and to Hold

I treasure our nights together
roaming through these empty hallways
your pithy kisses gently tread
like faint footfalls from seraphim
each swift embrace purloins my breath
a parasitic act for sure
one that I gladly tolerate
as a nostalgic remembrance

I'll collect the courage
to follow you someday
in your spectral half-life
but for now I'm content
with kisses from the past
swirling round like whispers

Not even in death do us part
My dear and sweet lover

Trick or Treat

November's gray and rainy days
have started a few days early
wet brown and orange leaves cling to you
like imps to their demonic lord
You let them scatter to the floor
greeting their fellow detritus
You pay them no heed as you sink
drowning into the davenport

From my voyeuristic
vantage I patiently
watch the mist gathering
into a formless mass
sending noxious tendrils
seeking your spinal chord

You swallow pills like candy corn
then greet your fellow wraiths

The Subliminal Lurker

It was a crisp autumn morning blanketed
with a light downy fog.
The maple and birch trees
donned in hues of yellow and orange
brought half a smile to my lips.

The ground still sodden
hinted back to those perpetual rain-riddled days
that had preceded this one
and which had made me miss
the gradual deciduous change.

So the vibrant shock of fire
through the smoke-like mist
captured my attention,
relieved my sodden soul,
brought a smile, or at least half a one, to my lips
and made me miss, in my inattention,
something else
something dire.

However, the jackdaws noticed.
Don't they always?
Like a swarm of giant gnats they flew to and fro
following their agitated alpha
in a chaotically choreographed contemporary dance
accompanied by insistent percussive caws.

What's got into them? I thought.

I go this way every morning,
never before had I seen the like
so their corvid fervor
awoke me from my reverie.

A chill wind began to rise
like a solo oboe melody creeping amongst the strings.
Dark clouds eclipsed the sun

marking the eventual return of the precipitation
that has flooded my being.

Like a hare fleeing a fox
my hasty heart palpitated.

And I knew
in my gut
in my soul
in the heart of my memory
it was here
behind me.

The dread of the unavoidable horror
had returned.
Gone was the smile, all be it only half a one.
Gone was the sheer autumnal joy.

Although I'll never see it,
not even in the corner of my eye,
I know the lurker is there
behind me
in the shadows,
in the cracks,
in the subliminal spaces
of my mind's eye.

So be it.

The corners of my mouth formed
half a rakish grin.

Let the lurker lurk.
I opened my umbrella
and continued toward my destination
without even an errant glance
over my shoulder.

Dream Ghost

You haunt me in my dreams
like a sucking lamprey
stealing vitae and mind
In my dreams I cannot
help but want to love you
as I once did before

Yet upon waking I regret
the day I willingly let you
sink psychic tendrils deep within
slowly eating with their barbed teeth
Even now freed from your clutches
I can still feel the sensation
of your leech-like nightmare caress
leaving my heart weak and weary

As I buried your corpse
I must entomb your hungry soul

No More

The first time you visited me
stepping sideways into my dreams
morphing nightly explorations
into ghastly grotesque nightmares,
I thought you were my animus
showing my own dingy mirror
a craving buried deep within
vices surpassed that I should love.

And I did cherish you
feeling I deserved you
my own warty boggart.
Your manipulation
of my dreams and desires
grew crueler over time.

I reave the cloak of your tortures
bound for the bless'd abyss.

Wild Spirits

I doubt that you despite your youth
have ever chanced to perceive us
as we flutter from tree to tree
but we have certainly seen you
because we are ever watchful
here in the heart of the forest
because we are ever alert
for a child's body to possess

You dance carefree under
the ancient oaks and pines
the homes of wild spirits
you scream and run with joy
because you have not seen
how we've gathered around

As I take over your physique
your feral soul roams free

Angst, Grief, Regret and Healing

Metamodern Morning Angst

My heart's bass drum back beat
joins the blaring alarm
a viper-like arm strikes
the beeping now *tacit*
the beats *rallentando*
softly *sotto voce*

Why can I not dream forever
like Alice in the looking glass
under the duvet air ripens
filling my soul with musty warmth
why can I not be forgotten
like lint in a jean's back pocket
out of my sight out of my mind
anxiety's cacophony

One eye surveys ahead
another stares inward appalled

Angst's Prisoner

Everyday when I wake
my heart races hoping
against all hope to rise
above all my struggles
Everyday I look out
the window of my mind
and glimpse upon wonders
folk and their normal lives

Children playing on the sidewalk
People rushing to work and school
Pigeons eating scraps left behind
I remember being like them
I remember life outside walls
created by the tyrant angst

Everyday my heart skips
hope's just a prisoner like me

The Prisoner

I don't know if she's a princess
a political prisoner
or an unruly teenaged brat
whatever the case she's locked up
in four-square meters of damp stone
Maybe its for her own damn good
or for the sake of the kingdom
whatever the case she shivers
the chill of public opinion

The mildew on the walls
like eternal despair
circles around the room
save for the lone window
where she sees a mocking
eagle's silhouette fly
above a long-dead ash

But it's cries of freedom ring false
mixed with raindrops of tears

An Elm in Spring

While winter's slumber chilled
throughout my sapwood veins
I dreamed of ages past
of children under shade
and women in their prime
orchestrating their lives

Yet through the veil of nostalgia
crept a thundering yearning gaze
that threatened to split me in twain
like Mjölnir striking a giant
The source a poor child's fantasy
fueled by anxiety and angst
and a strong desire to be seen
to emerge from its pupal husk

The sun's rays now lengthen
Look child — verdant buds awaken

Remember Me

I have blamed my Asperger's brain
for my lack of strong emotions
but there is probably something
happening behind the curtain
a frightened child alone sitting
shivering in a numb darkness
too afraid to hold out their hand
their emotional wall a sham

Ah to be like Dido with her
passion adamant resolute
a blazing bonfire's inferno
But ah one can never forget
her solemn chromatic descent
signing "When I am laid in earth"

Remember me, remember me!
But ah I can't repeat her fate

A Sonnet of Regret and Hope

I still hear the sharp ripping sound
of you tearing a shirt apart
a compulsion of frustration
arguing with a stubborn ass.
Frozen with my Asperger's mind
my stone-cliff face revealing nought
of the emotions hidden deep
beneath the obstinate facade.

The tangy berry scent
from your washed hair lingers
on my memory's pillow.
So I transform myself
to an open window
and invite your return

as time's breeze blows upon
the crumpled bedsheets of our lives.

Nightmare of Modern Life

Once again while charting
heavenly spheres all night
did my eyes softly close
just as Apollo rose
upon his chariot
of OxyContin bliss

Like Alice down the rabbit hole
my subconscious mind dared to roam
in the grand theater of our times
playing our enduring trouble
gelatinous coelenterates
float innocently here and there
on the stage all the while hiding
poisonous barbs that lie beneath

The mask of humane care
is a puppet of corporate greed

Recollections of a Wasp

At first I tried to free myself
from the sticky tree sap prison
that had ensnared my legs and wings
yet the more I struggled against
my fate the more fully encased
I became as the translucent
goo that enveloped my body
glistened in the light of the sun

Soon my vain struggling ceased
and my soul wandered through
the rock hard amber case
that had become my tomb
and how my soul did praise
its beauty and its grace

Alone I was a thing despised
Together we're a jewel

My Mother Was a Survivor

My mother was someone
who canned food and who saved
that which could be of use.
My mother was someone
who crocheted and who sang
lovely old-timey hymns.

My mother was a survivor
of the 20s' great depression
and the severe reality
of an insane planet at war.
My mother was a survivor
of humanity's scourge cancer
giving us extra time with her
although it was only borrowed.

So in the end cancer
would claim her body not her soul.

A Sonnet of Questions

Did my father hear the grim wail
of a banshee before he died?
Did he realize the ravaging
effect of chemotherapy
on a heart still cleaning up from
the hurricane gale of cancer?

Did he show regret for
things left unsaid undone
gone and lost forever
in the vacuum of time?
Did my absence bring doubt
about my love for him
a doubt whose dull silence
echoed across the sea?

These questions will always remain
exiled and unanswered

Just Four Ducks on a Pond

Nuclear family
two parents, two children
always harmonious
with bright smiles they gleam
like mallards on a pond
Instagram tells me so

My landmine-filled home is nothing
like those idyllic pastorals
that others post and boast about
instead we just try to survive
Yet there are ripples on the lake
hinting at some disturbances
hiding just below the surface
distorting their calm reflections

As a burnt-out parent
I empathize with the mallards

A Mother's Quest

Bound by my duties as mother
you would think nothing could
coax, quibble, convince me to leave
my home hearth and children
Yet the quest like a nautilus
drew me spiraling in
to the vortex of adventure
to save my dying son

Every parent faces trials
along the road of life
The obstacles strewn in my path
exasperated me
bureaucratic mumble jumble
and piles of paperwork
appeared like a Sphinx's riddles
or dragons to be slain

When my resolve turned to despair
like a vision from Zeus
Facebook's algorithms produced
a certain specialist
in experimental techniques
and CRISPR genetics
Of course our insurance refused
so I dug in to fight

With an attorney by my side
we proved that they should pay
for the gene-editing treatment
thus my son's life was saved

Today's Weather

The air is thickening
as if gathering up
moisture to make the rain
Birds still loudly gossip
like workers on a break
waiting out the tension

However, I sit here scribbling
thoughts in tune with the yellow grass
eagerly awaiting relief
a pregnant craving for water
Climate change's reality
has brought forth weeks of intense sun
slowly grinding down the living
between its fiery grindstone teeth

As the temperature drops
my yearning face turns toward the clouds

The Rise

Jet black darkness, the moonless sky's
patiently waiting for the sun
to scare away the absence of
color, brightness, and all things good
it's just an orb of gas and heat
yet the sight of this yellow ball
over the horizon can cause
oratorios in the throats
of bird and man alike
the symphony of dawn
as conducted by God
for the hearing of both
angel and man alike
all of the planets sing

Is it really a surprise that
I rejoice to greet her

Five Haiku Written in the Forest

Birdsong symphony
spreading gossip on the wind
proclaiming freedom

See how it scampers
industrious dorbeetle
slave to its nature

Verdant emerald touch
of the moss beneath my feet
I embrace solace

The wind whispers peace
into my awaiting ears
my shoulders unfold

Violet blueberries
whose blood stains all my fingers
noble sacrifice

At a Cabin in the Woods

Can you believe that on the edge of chaos lies stillness
    Zoom meetings, distance learning, viral fears can
        be forgotten
For here the air is filled with chattering songs and
    clearness

Leave behind work, stress and threat of illness
    Here the earthy aroma is musty yet not rotten
For on the edge of chaos lies stillness

At a simple cabin in the woods, the earth holds a rich-
    ness
    With the potential for treasures ungotten
All the while, the air is filled with whistling songs and
    clearness

The element that we seemingly avoid in town, placid
    tranquilness
    Combines with nature into a respite which can be
    gotten
Gratis, since on the edge of chaos lies stillness

Ah, to relax with coffee watching flitting blue tits eat
    with a fierceness
    That belies their form; yet they are not misbegotten
Just listen, the air is filled with their warbling songs
    and clearness

Shoes cast aside with the solar victory over chillness
    Lean back in the deck chair, clothed lightly in cot-
    ton
Yes, it's true, on the edge of chaos lies stillness
Finally my mind, like the air, is filled with chattering
    songs and clearness

A Sonnet of Healing

Cursing that blasted day
leaving behind comforts
and all those reminders
industrious black ants
building a hill piecemeal
in the devastation.

Leaving everything I enter
not meekly or in grave despair
but with an open mind I step
into the woods that lie within.
Finding solitude though birdsong
I feel your tenacious claws
releasing their firm vice-like grips.
Time slows. I straighten beaming bright.

The heart of the woods calls.
The past dissolves finally free.

Swallow Me Whole

The gossip of birdsong
lures me ever deeper
into your gaping mouth
devouring me with
blueberries dorbeetles
and fairy-ringed mushrooms.

The verdant emerald hues of green
surround me with your warm
and comforting blanket of moss
soft flannel pajamas of leaves.
Your breath speaks but one word to me
"rest" — for you know I am weary
like a diver ever deeper
feeling the weight of the water
of everything that lies above.

Here inside your belly
I float freely and rest in peace.

A Hope-filled Melody

There is more than crisis and tragedy
    A kind word aloud, rather than unsaid
One more note for a hope-filled melody

A young musician's thoughts are prosody
    Like a loom with heddles, yarn and some thread
There is more than crisis and tragedy

I know our world seems like a parody
    Mankind's heart leans pure, so don't be mislead
One more note for a hope-filled melody

Right now we are obsessed with malady
    Mankind will endure, and it will succeed
There is more than crisis and tragedy

Together we can make a remedy
    Morning dew and sunshine are guaranteed
One more note for a hope-filled melody

Nature's glory unbound is rhapsody
    A flowering bush ready to reseed
There is more than crisis and tragedy
One more note for a hope-filled melody

Change and Metamorphosis

So I'm a Gorgon, and That's Okay

I awoke one morning to the squirming of my hair, as
      if it was trying
to slither away of its own accord. Naturally, I felt that
      was rather odd.
So I slid out of bed and performed all the usual morn-
      ing rituals
before looking into the mirror only to find that not
a single strand of my luxuriant black hair was there,
      replaced by a nest of snakes, what kind
I didn't know — something poisonous, no doubt.

Which is something that you probably feel right now,
      doubt.
However, I need you to try
to understand that there was a basis for this happen-
      ing, this was not some kind
of hoax and nothing was odd
or strange about it. People already avoided my gaze,
      having learned not
to look at me when I'm overcome with with ticks or fail
      to perform my rituals.

The frustration that explodes from me during an in-
      terrupted ritual
is not something that you want to experience, nor my
      paralyzing glare. So doubt
all you want. I've always known the gorgon within,
      whose obsessive thoughts cannot
be turned away so easily. God knows I've tried.
Yet the little repeated behavior does help for the odd
few seconds to keep the pressure cooker of stress from
      an explosion of some kind.

I do my best to be kind
and to fit in this perfect Instagram world. My rituals,
although they seem odd,
are a needed coping mechanism. There is no doubt

that I'm trying.
It's just that I fail more often than not.

So these snakes were not
something new, a new kind
of trial or torture trying
to destroy those in my sight. Like the rituals
that must be performed, I doubt
not that I own these beasts too, however odd.

So I will name them each in their odd
fashion whether you like it or not:
Anxiety born of doubt,
Remorse for all those frustrating failures of kindness,
Compulsion the force behind all rituals,
and Resignation in knowing that day after day one
        must continue trying.

Now there is no doubt in my mind that I am not odd
or whatever freakish label you try to place on me, and
        I'm most certainly not
a monster, that some hero beheads, instead of kindly
        looking beyond this and all my rituals.

The Metamorphosis

This may sound unbelievable
but my daughter metamorphosed
during the night and awakened
to the slithering of her hair
her once luxurious dun locks
were now a nest of writhing snakes
vitriolic viperidae
each unique of hue and design

We soon learned to avoid
her terrifying glare
which under bouts of rage
could petrify your heart
so misunderstandings
are now fraught with peril

We will not summon Perseus
for we are gorgons too

Decay

The first thing I noticed
was half a fingernail
hanging ready to fall
dangling ready to spin
like a helicopter
maple seed in the wind

things then deteriorated
your fingers and toes empty husks
like the partially decayed leaves
strewn round as mulch before winter
and yet you seemed unaffected
by the leper-like erosion
since your neurodiverse mind flowed
through the white rapids of your thoughts

My own diverse neurons
seek patterns in your mulch-laced hands

Fungal Sublimation

I woke up yesterday
With a turquoise-blue fuzz
Growing between my toes
Producing a constant
Satisfying sharp itch
That roused an ancient soul

For within that sublime prickle
An injection of DNA
An exchange of information
Of millennia long since passed
A sensation of belonging
The return of a wondering
Prodigal spawn into the fold
Deconstructed into oneness

Thus transformed my body
Wears Gaia's turquoise-blue mantle

Winter Was Hard

Winter was hard a cold dagger
wedged deep between my subconscious
and the nightmarish facts of war
winter was hard a blow against
the Faberge ego I'd spent
a lifetime sculpting into clay

Now when March has tantrums
stubbornly refusing
to let timid April
leave the depths of my heart
the remaining coldness
propagates in my blood
threatening to destroy
my virus-weakened soul

Winter was hard a grim glacier
before whom wc rcpcnt

Spring's Return

Although I cannot join
my heart transforms itself
into a fleeting moth
'pon seeing spring's return
women going about
and children at their play

Although the moth stretches its wings
ice-like amber entraps its soul
what tethers me so securely
that I cannot open the door
the ghost of a hard winter preys
upon my insecurities
anxiety's undead corpse rises
a malevolent guardian

Yet the ice starts to crack
seeing branches with verdant buds

Awaiting Persephone

As the sky turns a livid blue
to contrast the unblemished snow
we are compelled to speculate
that Persephone's fierce quarrels
have been inadequate to sway
winter's cold plutonian heart
whose icy ivy-like tendrils
are foredoomed yet still holding fast

So every year we long
for Sol's lengthening rays
to awaken frozen
yet germinating seeds
we long for her agile
pirouetting dance steps

Listen crocuses are blooming
her harbingers arrive

March

There's a state of limbo
between the depression
of desolate winter
and the warming smiles of
crocuses and lilies
in April's turbulence

If you look into the faces
of the people who pass you by
you will surely see some sad souls
undergoing purgatory
their minds struggling like Sisyphus
pushing their emotional stones
hoping to someday reach the sun
crocuses buried in the snow

The sky is still livid
when the trees have begun to bud

Spring in Sweden

The spring sun burns brightly
Though the trees still lack buds
Winter was long and hard
Our patience brings rewards
As warblers warble their
Joy at the warming
Rays that give hope to all
Who choose to bask and bathe

The ground soaked with half-melted snow
Between frozen rock-hard winter
And hydroless summer dust
Holds within itself the power
Of rebirth Persephone's gift
Making me smile despite the muck

I plant a seed of hope
Not knowing what the future brings

The Symphony of Spring

The robin announces
the arrival of spring
with a flurry of chirps
as the ever warmer
ever delightful sun
shines over its shoulder

Part of this morning symphony
of such glorious proportions
is a hidden inner message
which one must listen carefully
a counterpoint of exquisite
subtlety and superb technique
that only with one's heart and soul
can this proclamation be heard

What does the herald cry
Why love, life, and your arrival

A Time of Change
(for Åsa-Marie)

Summer stretched long and bountiful
bright smiles and strawberry memories
sun-kissed lilacs and irises
lifted our spirits for awhile
newly-plucked blueberry smoothies
the sharp sweet smell of fresh-cut grass
smoke and sparks rising from the grill
formed a false sense of permanence

For as the sun's rays wane
lignon berries replace
their indigo sisters
lilies of the valley
wither into heather
earth's wool-woven sweater

While cherishing summer memories
we fondly look ahead

Cosmic Horrors

A Curse Upon the Land

When we purchased the farm
under the sunless gaze
of bleak January,
little did we suspect
that nothing would grow here
save your vampiric lust.

What fiendish, far-flung star spawned you,
and brought a curse upon the land?
Our crops have withered on the vine,
dust-filled caricatures of life.
The goats saw you for what you are
and ran off rather than despair.
And yet we remain, your good thralls,
bound by our ashen-snow-filled minds.

Your nuclear winter
absorbs our souls to set yours free.

Addiction

I've tried to stay away,
such an electric drug,
our symbiotic dance.
First fatigue smacks me hard
after being with you
then power, pure essence.

You seem to know when I am weak
unable to resist sweet gifts.
Strength pours in me with every drop
that you graciously bestow me.
Hating myself my obsession
which hopelessly degrades us both.
Our bodies orbit each other
locked with a pregnant gravity.

Did we ever once love?
Your blood and mine become as one?

When I Joined the Living Dead

I should not have been there
but I took a shortcut
hurrying for a date
naturally I got mugged
my slashed artery gushed
like a champaign fountain

In shock my mind danced in and out
gracefully between their lush screams
after the crying chorus dimmed
a decorous voice sang to me
—hush my child it will soon be done
her rakish beauty transfixed me
nailed me upon a crucifix
as she siphoned my life essence

I exist in limbo
neither living nor truly dead

Climate Change

The month of April passed
without any showers
elf tears do not suffice
so May flowers struggle
where shall bees and faeries
flit and pirouette now

Plastic iron radio waves
proud symbols of mankind's progress
modern wards to keep the fae at bay
letting us safely watch TikTok
somewhere a puckish garden grows
a refuge from technology
and its child metamodern angst
far from this dull castle and cage

Please accept this offering
my soul yearns for rain's kind caress

The Chosen One

Tonight is the summer solstice
My day, oh blessed lord, my night
It's the longest day of the year
Yet the stars twinkle like dew drops
Covering the fiddlehead ferns
Here in her woods, the Mother's place
I am the chosen one, the key
Thousands of her young shall be born

My skin is glorified
With the arcane etchings
Needed for opening
The gate, the bridge, the world
Soon she shall reign supreme
I smile in my role

As midnight approaches
Moonlight reflects on the knife's edge

Answering the Call

What color do you think
is the heart of the woods
verdant green crimson noir
as it pulsates softly
bass drum obbligato
beckoning demanding

Like a courting beau it bestows
largesse that merges with my soul
granting me bestial insight
from both predators and their prey
It's an unrelenting suitor
patience of the oak waiting for
my inescapable escape
from the asylum my prison

My heart joining the drum
shackleless answering the call

The Heart of the Forest

I can see you plucking
blueberries while swatting
the ever annoying
mosquitos and horse flies
cursing stooping laughing
snubbing the forest's call

Eventually I see you pause
with a plump berry in your hand
royal violet fingers moving
toward your mouth — I weep 'cause I know
I know what will, what must happen
I can see you rising slowly
like a morning fiddlehead fern
before entering the bracken

I can see you merging
foliage and flesh now as one

That Which Lies Waiting

Your kind has always come
noisily tramping with
high hope for a bounty
chanterelle, blueberries
black raspberries and more
auras glowing with greed

Your only thoughts — what you can take
announce your presence long before
the disturbances of your limbs
their thoughts awaken my slumber
for they are intone with my own
and a ravenous hunger grows
If these woods now seem strange shifting
you must follow the paths I make

Deep in the forest's heart
you'll feed me with your greed

The Forest Wife

Ratta tat ratta tat
the woodpecker's message
morse-coded just for me
adds to the cuckoo's call
they're insistent these birds
too long I've ignored them

Even the squirming of the ants
whose fluidly forming patterns
pierce my brain like the banshee's wail
as I cover my ears and scream
The message is plain and simple
—In the heartwoods they've been waiting
waiting years for me to return
where dryads and huldras roam free

Sorrow joy and tears dance
as I turn my back toward my young

The Lab Rat

One February doleful day
with an aged cognac in my hand
I studied with a fixation
rivaled only by those near death
when my wall of Jericho fell
not to the bleating of ram's horns
but to the incessant thunder
of your fist rapping at my door

My studies now train wrecked
cast a foul mien upon
the face that greeted you
that was warning enough
but like a dim raven
you heedlessly barged in

Vital research must continue
on your suitable soul

Halloween Feast

A nearly full moon rises high
beaming proudly like a parent
because *samhain* is upon us.
The crisp, electric atmosphere
brings the essence of pumpkin leaves
to my senses with just a hint
of something more desirable
awakening a memory
ancient, eternal as longing.

Changed are the festive sounds
now mostly of children
laughing and saying "boo!"
But still they don clothing
in a feeble attempt
to ward off one like me.

The elder signs are vanquished, gone.
Tonight I feast again.

Symphony in Yellow

The opening movement
with screeching woodwind gulls
mimes the scene of Wilde's quay.
Yet the yearning duet
cello and bass trombone
reflects a darker source.

The inner movements raise a fog
hued of sunflower maize and amber.
As the harmonic interplay brings
anticipation fruition
the return of the sovereign.
The final *vivace* races.
Frantically invoking brass
puncture straight through reality.

A path to Carcosa
now opens for the tattered king.

We Ghouls

Halloween is finally here.
We are nearly, yet not quite free
free to dance the dance macabre.
For tonight we leave our grottos
with drool dripping from gruesome jaws
as the moon wanes and the bonds break.
Let's begin the time of harvest
for the devourer below.

The food must not be fresh
fetid like a ripe mold
holding inside itself
the power to decay
and to rejuvenate
the circle unbroken.

For the devourer demands
we ghouls fill its larder.

Hive Mind (ketek)

Serving glorious royalty
we contentedly join
the hive,
the joint contentedness
we royally, gloriously serve

Starry Night

It is Walpurgis Night
star- and moonshine twinkle
through the glass-like ether
Below me in the cleavage
between the ancient hills
lies the town and its church.

But tonight is Walpurgis Night
their god's hold on reality
wanes moon-like with each passing hour
while primordials awaken
an eldritch distortion begins
twisting both matter and ether
remaking the world into that
which she the blessed one can tread

One final glance above
reveals the brush strokes of a god

A Fateful Midsummer

This year for midsummer
we fled north to Lapland
to praise the midnight sun
Naked and free we danced
morning cloak butterflies
we worshiped with the wind

We believed our festivities
would amuse the mother goddess
who would honor us with a boon
forgetfulness by nepenthe
for our souls carry the boulders
pestilence famine war and death
under whose encumbrance we pine

No boon she brings but bane
a rough beast slouching from the east

The Sinner's Prayer

Oh Lord, oh Lord, what have I done?
    Can you please forgive me
while I'm still on the run?

I can't blame anyone
    but myself, don't you see?
Oh Lord, oh Lord, can you forgive what I have done?

She was the chosen one
    The bridge, gate and key
How long must I remain on the run?

Donned in glyph-embroidered vestment so finespun
    in order to greet the great god soon to roam free
Oh Lord, oh Lord, I can't bear what I have done

Her sanguine hair glistened in the sun
    as the others chanted with abandoned glee
Right before I'd soon be forced to run

A blast from my shotgun
    like the eerie wailing of a banshee
Oh Lord, oh Lord, what have I done?
Please, help this poor sinner on the run

Custer's Last Stand

For weeks we and the Lakota
have been dreaming of massacres
with soldiers falling like insects
before the devourer below
They will surely gather forces
The greasy grass shall be a trap
Hundreds of men and animals
delivered and slaughtered for us

For my clan has gathered
Our shaman has foretold
we will revel and feast
now the stars have aligned
The devourer demands
its larder should be filled

We ghouls serve our god and master
Custer shall be dessert

Invisibility

I've learned how to hide in shadows
practically invisible
as I hurry to my next class
hugging myself against the walls
the gazes of other students
impotently ricochet off
small hailstones against the window
they hardly touch and never stay

With this new-found power
my ship cruises through life
avoiding any harm
a child never seen
nor heard by another
till seated at my desk

When I finally graduate
no one will remember

Last Night I Dreamed of Cthulhu

Last night I dreamed of Cthulhu
sitting asymmetrically
upon a mammoth basalt throne
patiently abiding his time
flitting all around like midges
were numerous grotesque mermen
court stewards of this drowned chateaux
serving under his dominion

My racing heart transfixed
skipping a beat or two
pierced me to consciousness
my unfit tortured mind
creaked bent into angles
that would drive Euclid mad

Glimpsing cosmic preeminence
I'll humbly serve the call

Lodger at the Witch House

As a child I drank Mother's milk
every Imbolc and Lughnasadh
until I manifested blood
with each season my powers grew
like a wolf's moon ever waxing
my manifold maturity
should possess sufficient power
yet it betrays my heart's intent

Candlemas is coming
my polymath lodger
the angles of your mind
shine ferociously dark
which Euclid could not dare
holding Pandora's key

I-ä, i-ä, Shub-niggurath!
you shall return at last

A Newly Awoken Wiccan

A newly awoken Wiccan
borrowed the eyes hawks and deer
and the touch of moss following
incautious footsteps on the loam
as a procession of a sect
lead her beguiled friend to doom
for his mathematical genius
could shatter time's acute angles

She called on Mother Earth
and Father Nodens too
thus a homely vessel
she filled with their power
incandescent she strode
into their loathsome glade

A newly awoken Wiccan
would stop a god that day

Solving the P'naptuk Paradox

Oh Mother with a thousand spawn
I beseech you to awaken
from eternal hibernation
awaken and reclaim your throne
Queen of the night Queen of shadows
this young man's mathematical mind
solves the P'naptuk paradox
the gate beckoningly opens

Hear his mutterings
as they echo through time
like Noah's turtledoves
or a crushed butterfly
sending wavelets through time
embrittling your shackles

The anointed athame waits
the riddle's solution

The Fractured Ceremony

The Hollow was being ravaged
roaming bands of reavers
struck terror among gentlefolk
scattering bloodstone tears
"The old gods have abandoned us"
the acolytes decried
silvered tongues dripping nothingness
suffering and sorrow

They promised to move the planet
through eldritch rituals
The new gods will be ferocious
they will keep us from harm
The ceremony went awry
sonorous slashing steel
interrupting the sombre chants
till silence reigned supreme

At once our world was cut in twain
now neither here nor there
Two universes both vying
splintered coalescence
Divinities novel and old
Marched one foot in each realm
Manifestly ineffective
in both curses and boons

Yet the fractured ritual like
the mountain snow thawing
cleared a celestial passage
for louche monstrosities

A Father's Song

Slithering through the walls
your voices reach my heart
like a blooming spore cloud
tokens and mementos
Deep in my heart's blackhole
that swirling sorrow-filled
void flow my tears with them

When our world was splintered in twain
you were stuck on the other side
like the veil between life and death
once you cross never to return
Ignorant and lacking the means
to traverse the veil and join you
I am torn in two like our realm
knowing you are both near and far

My joyous mournful song
Hope slithering its way toward you

Mirror Mine

My twin and I were born
at the precise moment
two universes merged
I was born to this world
while my dusky sister
leans toward the eldritch realm

Yet she completes me, my mirror
We are piebald shadows and light
cast from a tired sun through the trees
shifting patterns making a whole.
Yet her dark presence terrifies
our fellow villagers, minds closed
unable to see what we are
gathering now to make things "right."

Mirror mine, follow me.
We'll step with one foot in each world.

Caged

Somehow the creature in the cage
using only the fiery
fierce blueness of its feral eyes
a powerful leaden yearning
plowed roughshod through my trembling heart
Before reason could intervene
money and pleasantries exchanged
the contents and the cage were mine

Each night I lose myself
wandering the vast wilds
that lie within those orbs
whose gaze holds cryptic truths
locked forever beyond
mystic cypher I lack

Each night I find myself
locked behind cold cobalt-blue bars

After the Fall

There were planet tremors
forest fires and storms
thoughts of the world ending
In the streets rioters
pillaged like enemy
soldiers within our gates

You tucked me away for safety
dying defending all our wares
now only detritus dross junk
You were a moth drawn toward the flames
Following the wake of chaos
to fill the bleeding hole you left
came a monster my new master
with tendrils bored into my brain

I am now its puppet
yearning to be free, safe and dead

Speculative Poems and Other Musings

Salvage

Parsecs from the nearest system
with an inelegant
pitch and yaw botched cabriolé
swiveled the Fitzgerald

Ingesting chaff and detritus
like bats eating midges
our scavenger drones cleared the way
for me and my shipmates

Engineer sent some of the drones
whose subtle caresses
retarded the wild pirouette
allowing us to dock

With the climate control long dead
we didn't even fear
encountering bacteria —
the sterile kiss of space

An explosion inside the bridge
had blasted through the hull
ridding the bridge of air and crew
gifting them to the void

The containment seals on each door
would eventually leak
making the ship a lifeless hulk
or so it seemed to us

A dark silent and empty ship
with limited salvage
unless the cargo held treasure
to make it all worthwhile

The cargo hold was cramped and tight
so we let the loader

transfer all the trunks and cases
until it revealed a great prize

Organic strands and filaments
a comforting cocoon
hid the pupa of a young queen
whom we must now protect

We serve a higher purpose now
delivering our charge
our thoughts and hers are now as one
as our ship warps back home

Seeds from Space

As we crawl through the slippery clay
looking more like insects
than genetically enhanced men
my mind reflects upon
the sheer folly of our mission
we are the invaders
we are the aliens from space
the creatures of nightmares
a foil rallying the natives
to defend their planet

A barren planet we were told
just oversee the drones
and machines that will terraform
the rock into heaven
the lifeless seas and dust-filled plains
would grow ever verdant
under our benevolent care
laying the foundation
for a writhing horde of settlers
to people the planet

We did not realize that life grows
in the interior
in the cavernous vastness there
our boring and mining
awoke their curiosity
we didn't notice them
but we noticed the things they did
looting and destroying
all our equipment gone in hours
to defend their planet

We are herded under the ground
by amorphous shadows
we descend helpless but with awe

for their uncanny world
invaders to feed their planet

Eternity

The survey drones found that
a colossus remains
whose alien visage
mimics the pride of man
and whose four monstrous arms
hold curious symbols

A flame to inspire or burn?
A scythe for harvest or for war?
A chain for bonds or for bondage?
A hammer to build or to slay?
Nanobots clean, polish, repair
So the poisonous winds cannot
Erode those grotesque frowning lips
Or dull the sparkling of its eyes
Forever the giant must gleam

Yet the survey's results
show that the sphere is without life

Tale of the Nebra Sky Disk

Deep in sleep for thousands of years
a disk of turquoise-hued copper
found itself on the black market
a thing to be traded away
so it connected with the sky
and the sleeping gods that dwell there
therein the gods infiltrated
the stark dreams of Harald Meller

The heavenly bodies
now gleam with a golden
radiance that rivals
their pure cosmic models
an elegant brillance
contrasting the green sky

Why is it still not satisfied?
no solstice does it greet

Saintly Motion

The sun will rise today
'tis a statement of fact
a certainty of life
with her perfect circle
the celestial orb glides
through the ether of space

However here it is dark and
no amount of guarantee can
keep one's faculty of reason
from postulating the myst'ries
that surround, circumvent daily
existence to the extent that
even the heavenly spheres might
fail in their eternal duty

Of course such heresy
will undo me long before then

Entering the Sublime

The year after the pandemic
we opened the sublime gateway
thus members of the exalted
could pass into the worlds beyond
We'd just barely stopped the disease
by turning our home world to dust
since the next one might finish us
we eagerly left our bodies

No more pain and sorrow
Fear and greed abandoned
we joined the infinite
a singular oneness
pure energy and thought
glimpsing the face of god

Who knew the solution would be
cultural suicide

Some Philosophical Pondering Over the Nature of Fate

Orpheus sat at a tiny cafe his golden lyre upon his lap
—She'll be here any minute now he thought while
    throwing a glance or two his watch
—Would you like to order something while you wait
    for madame to arrive
—Sure a glass of ice tea would be nice
—Is that all
—For now

    (singing)
I once loved a woman
whose lunar like eyes did
hold my heart as if caged
I once loved a woman
I know not why nor did
I care such was my youth

—Ah thank you

Philosophers and poets can
argue day by day over the
esoteric qualities of
the nature of ultimate truth
They quarrel and haggle over
the ultimate question of life
the universe and everything
and yet they could not answer this

I once loved a woman
I know not why nor did I care

—A note sir from madame
—Oh thank you

    (reading)
```
Orph, I'm leaving you.  Your constant
        singing
and plucking have really gotten on my
```

```
          nerves.
Hope you understand.

Eurydice
```

—Ah . . .
—Yes sir
—Ahhhh . . .
Check please

The Tale of Perseus and Medusa

Do you know what really happened
when Perseus was sent to slay
poor old Medusa in her lair?
Was she really so hideous
that eye contact with her could kill?
Was her reputation tarnished
by lecherous men of power
a me too victim of regret?

Perhaps fair Perseus
was invited for tea
maybe he was dazzled
by Chrysaor's beauty
riding Pegasus home
holding each other tight

Definite answers will come forth
just listen to her voice

The Fate of the Party

We had been on the trail
of a rare hippogriff
when we stumbled upon
a dulled marble sculpture
whose uncanny visage
was locked in a grimace
so atrociously vile
we nearly lost our breath

"Who'd shape stone in such a manner?"
the priest among us faired to ask
" 'Twas the tooth of the basilisk"
the elven magician decreed
The dwarven scout spat tobacco
"It is Medusa's handy work"

One by one they all died
but being blind I fell in love

Life Goes On

I'm finally heading home
in this freezing, ceaseless winter
just a bit past the former police station
which is now a burnt-out shell, pretty much like ev-
      erything
else from my former life
I try not to dwell on the past but not too hard

Since the blast crippled us, life's been hard
especially here at home
where we're all just trying to survive, but life,
you know, just goes on through this never-ending
      winter
and we are like everything
equals all of the same station

I crank the handle on my radio, but I can't find a sta-
      tion
keep thinking some smart person will start broadcast-
      ing, it can't be that hard
but they all went out like everything
else around this place I call home
where there is shelter from the storms of winter
and where life goes on, yes, life

Look here peaking through the snow — life
crocuses right beside the station
crocuses used to mean that spring was dispelling win-
      ter
in the old days it didn't seem so hard
to endure the cold and darkness at home
but now things are hard, most things, no, everything

put down the scrounged wood and food and remember
      everything
about life
at home
a little past the station

before things became so hard
and the winter

before the never-ending winter
put such a strain on everything
making even the simplest task hard
yet there is life
here just past the police station
home

even with nuclear winter there is still life
and the hope that everything will return to its natural
        station
but it's becoming so hard just to leave my home

By Candlelight

Dance on little flame; yes dance on
for who can guess when you will drown
in a murky pool of melted
wax melted via your own heat
Dance on oh little flame; dance on
for at any second a gust
could bluster over you eating
away all of your oxygen

For you see I'm content
to sit here watching you
with your graceful footfalls
You are truly beauty
personified on earth
and I'm awed by your glow

Dance on my little flame; dance on
by your light darkness flees

Innocence Lost

the babe cries for his mom
yearning for the only
comfort that they can know
searching for completion
of all their desires
in the bosom of love

how peculiar that the more we
prosper and mature the more we
revert to an age of lesser
complexity with its simpler
needs and wants and its well defined
terms of fulfillment and pleasure
an age that we left willingly
perhaps even though fear made us

to replace the bosom
I hold my hand out in the dark

Two Sonnets Smothered with Marmalade

It was Ursula
        the wise old woman of Earthsea
                Hain
                Portland Oregon
        and other mystical locales

                        who taught me

        how to shed my pride

in order to
        hold my hand out in the dark

                        What else can you do?

Yet she didn't fully

        explain to me
                        the procedure for healing

        after I had become
                        a man whose hand was shot off
        I nearly bled to death

I

*The wound left scar tissue
on my arm and my mind
The healing process failed
to make me whole like new
Now on cold winter nights
the pain revisits me*

*I am now over protective
of my remaining useful hand
Layers of fortifications
serve to keep out any new pains
You see I've learned my lesson well*

during the wars that rocked my soul
It is hard to be burned when one
avoids hot ovens and fires

Now on cold winter nights
I'm reminded of what I lost

So you see I called

her up via a spell, like a seance,
            and the Mother replied

—Tis (that's TS pronounced like a word) you have to pick
yourself up.
—I know but it's so hard to do
—Nonsense you have the strength
—What will happen to me after that

II

I'm blind well not really
but I've darkened my specs
to the impaired threshold
You see I'm too gutless
to ram a knife into
my face can't stand the pain

I'm blind (I've explained that before)
so I've spent my life wandering
groping through the mist like darkness
that engulfs my sight and my soul
However every now and then
an object with a radiance
that shines with such intense brightness
that even impaired as I am

Its splendor can I see
As I hold my hand out to it

The elder paused

        shrouding me with her

silence
        a silence that calmed

        my troubled mind

—What can you do . . .

        She finally spoke as her words

             sliced into my psyche
          as a laser
        burning into a tumor

— . . . but hold your other hand out in the dark
—And if I lose that hand also
—One must have faith in the inherent kindness in people. Who knows maybe you'll find a kindred spirt.
—Kindred spirit?

Five-card Set: The Fool, The Hermit Reversed, Temperance, The Moon, and The Sun

In my twenties I would often
go dancing always with the hope
that this time I would meet someone
with x-ray eyes a lightning smile
patiently with each rejection
I accepted my hermitage
knowing that my Asperger shield
turned me invisible to all

Breaking routine felt like
Sisyphus and his stone
but on my friend's advice
I reentered the world
without desire or thought
as I basked in moonlight

my subconscious mind opened by
your sun-like radiance

Cow Tippin'

I'm from Wayne County Ohio
throw a stone and you'll likely hit
a farmer or at least a cow
One thing you have to understand
that there is nothing much to do
for teens on a Saturday night

So hopefully you will
forgive our teenaged selves
for being dumb and bored
and a bit gullible
That inevitably
driving on dirt back roads
someone would always say
—Hey let's go cow tippin'

The cows were locked up in their barns
and not a one was tipped

Summer's End

The sky falls in torrents
upon aborted plans
The freedom of summer
slowly erodes away
before the dark specter
of our career's millstone

If one had a basic income
universally guaranteed
allowing a more flexible
balance between one's life and work
for the pursuit of happiness
is a right bestowed upon us
a right drowning in the torrent
from capitalistic storm clouds

What wondrous creations
our metamorphosis would bare

Faithful

Now it's Friday again
porridge bubbles and plops
oat-filled molten magma
a comforting routine
against the loneliness
of gray December days

Predictably after breakfast
he wanders, careful not to slip
on the snow-covered ice puddles
that life has bestowed on his path
Poseidon's call urges him on
as he unerringly avoids
the few well-wrapped adventurers
between him and his goal the quay

What boon does he request
as the gulls feast upon his soul?

The Cat in the Bag

Here I am in a sack
My leisurely napping
rudely interrupted
my glorious dreaming
of hunts won and hunts lost
crumbling away from me

Why on earth would some fool human
lift up a tranquil, sleeping cat
then unceremoniously
dump her into a crude cloth bag?
No doubt some nefarious plan
rather hasty and ill conceived
the preposterousness of it
riles up my gall into a hiss

Now as the bag opens
claws extend to embrace chaos

A Metamodern Ballade

Yesterday my love disappeared
into the nexus hub
shimmering like ions in rain
which left an afterglow
in the retina of my mind
a grim sublime gesture
whether meant as a grand f-you
or passive aggressive
I don't know but the impression
became a metaphor

Yesterday I was born again
a rebooted system
devoid of cruft with a cleared cache
I wandered anew as a cloud
of newly stored data
stable yet seemingly shifting
a sea of silicon
a resplendently shimmering
adamantium mask
became a metaphor

Yesterday you battered the sprawl
your amphetamine smile
cutting through the capitalist dream
like a monowire string
personal neon announcements
algorithmically shot
bounced off your oxycontin shield
nothing could slow you down
a weaving psychic juggernaut
became a metaphor

Yesterday a narcissist used
nostalgia fetish
to justify his impudence
for those suckling the teats

of the ghost of Shub-Niggurath
a savior ascending
tilting against paper Nazis
forging the past's mythos
blossoms glowing in homespun praise
became a metaphor

Yesterday the metaverse died
under the sheer weight of
metamodern anxiety
postmodern irony
collapsed beside the Twin Towers
the utopian dreams
of us Gen Xers liquified
with the polar icecaps
which is why Greta Thunberg
became a metaphor

Tomorrow our society
will enter the sublime
leaving behind a legacy
ranging from angst to hope
thus becoming a metaphor

Old Magics

In the edge of the woods
there is a sun-draped glade
where rosemary and sage
spearmint and mistletoe
play amongst irises
in druidical bliss

From an Elysian cabin
emerge a woman and a man
together the caretakers bless
their herbs, vegetables and flowers
with a magical infusion
of devotion and nurturing
designed to deny the slowly
emerging darkness of the night

Yet what can old magics
do in the face of tyranny?

Awestruck

Our light-polluted sky
did little to prepare
me and my feeble mind
for the staggering
beauty incandescing
outside my porthole view
in the reaches of space

Gas and debris like cosmic cliffs
the Carina Nebula roars
with void-filling voiceless thunder
that only elder gods can hear
but I can see its majesty
and the sight fills the emptiness
tenderly lightens the burden
of my earthly mortality
and grants a taste of the sublime

My heart smiled knowing that
immortality can be brief

Playing Shostakovich's Fifth Symphony, a Bass Trombonist's Perspective

Warming Up

There is an unusual excited tension the air, even though the tuba player is cracking jokes with the tenors and me, as if this was just any afternoon concert. Yet behind the laughter, a cool professionalism mans our psyches as we focus for the task at hand—to do justice to the survivor of the great purge, Shostakovich and his Fifth Symphony. The door to the green room opens, and we, like tuxedoed black ants, file out to our seats. The audience in the concert hall reacts to the tension with acute anticipation. We tune and wait, eyes on the baton as it rises. It is time.

First Movement—Moderato

Life vacillating
between string-sweet calmness
pregnant with the threat from
the sudden synchronized
ponderous power of
tuba and bass trombone.

I wonder if symphonies can
be autobiographical.
Still periods of harmony
are interrupted by chaos,
the threat of censor, and the purge
that destroyed or banished thousands.
Discord and respite alternate
as in Shostakovich's life.

Must I revel playing
bass trombone as the party's sword?

Second Movement—Allegretto

Concessions to conform
are a constant in life.

Why would Shostakovich
be any different?
Or is this ironic
patriotic whimsy?

The hero and the symphony
parade unashamedly dressed
in socialistic uniforms
seeking approval from Stalin.
How can we portray the tightrope
the symphony dances upon?
How should I nuance the timbre
vibrating from my soul and horn?

I feel that bass trombone
is Dmitri's ironic voice.

Third Movement — Largo

Children of the cold war
had restless nights and dreamed
apocalyptic dreams.
Those dread-filled nightmares were
my chance to empathize
with those in the Great Purge.

The heavy fustiness clinging,
like rain droplets on a petal,
to the atmosphere of his time
percolated a bitter brew.
Conform to the majority
risk compunction and contrition.
Explore the unknown of genius
risk denouncement, detainment, death.

Tacet trombones regard
greatness achieved by mixing both.

Fourth Movement — Allegro non troppo

> The hero has returned.
> Cacophonous fanfare
> implies internal strife.
> The true antagonist
> for a great composer—
> desire for acceptance.
>
> Thundering triumphs are replaced
> with solemn, string-lead melodies
> that reflect a tense harmonic
> requiring resolution.
> Neither defeat nor victory
> emerge from the chord progressions.
> Instead the hero has claimed both,
> a disentangled dissonance.
>
> The struggle does not end
> but lives on to be played again.

Applause

Like a heavy late August rain, plump particles of applause and cheers descend and splash upon us. As if sensing the simile, large beads of sweat drip down my forehead. Their saltiness burns my eyes, while I stand proudly holding my bass trombone at attention in front of me, looking out into the sea of faces. Both audience and the performers celebrate a masterwork written as a reaction to Stalin's disapproval of earlier works, yet neither can comprehend such greatness, such genius. We can only try to fulfill the artist's response to "just" criticism.